Quotes
– on –
Character

Quotes
– on –
Character

" "

Inspirational Words on Courage,
Leadership, and Creativity

Tael –
a little
inspiration
for you!
Best,
mc

COMPILED BY M.C. SUNGAILA

Crystal Cove
PRESS

Published by Crystal Cove Press®, Newport Beach, California

Edited and designed by Girl Friday Productions
www.girlfridayproductions.com

Design: Paul Barrett
Project management: Katherine Richards

ISBN (paperback): 978-1-7338657-4-6
LCCN: 2020916435

To my parents, who encouraged a love of words

Contents

• • • • • • • • • •

Preface

• • • • • • • •

Ihave collected inspiring quotes since college, inscribing them into journals and scrawling them on Post-it Notes on my computer. Their sources are many: the Bible, classic literature, newspaper articles and interviews, and even podcasts and Twitter posts.

This book represents a collection of these quotes, centered on the theme of individual character.

Strength of character is the foundation of strong individuals and communities, and a fulfilling life. This book is organized around these guideposts: belief, courage, determination, leadership, love, meaningful work, creativity, joy, and independence.

I hope they inspire you to become the best you can be and, in turn, to share your best with others.

M.C. Sungaila
Newport Coast, California
July 2020

Belief

• • • • •

It is my task, my calling, my responsibility as a human being to find compassion for all forms of life. Through this I am more deeply connected to others and to the web of creation, the source of the thread that guides us and leads us home.

—Lauren Artress

• •

An honest man's the noblest work of God.

—Alexander Pope

It is important to expect nothing, to take every experience, including the negative ones, as merely steps on the path, and to proceed.

—Ram Dass

Do not allow evil to prevail, instead prevail over evil by means of goodness.

—Romans 12:21 (Catholic Public Domain Version)

• •

Now faith is the substance of things hoped for, the evidence of things not seen.

—Hebrews 11:1 (King James Version)

YOU ALREADY KNOW. THE SPIRIT IS WITH YOU AND THE SPIRIT IS IN YOU.

—Inspired by John 14:17

Pursue a righteous life—a life of wonder, faith, love, steadiness, courtesy. Run hard and fast in the faith. Seize the eternal life, the life you were called to, the life you so fervently embraced in the presence of so many witnesses.

—1 Timothy 6:12 (Message Bible)

I believe in the possibility of everything.

—Hope Edelman

• •

EACH OF YOU HAS BEEN BLESSED WITH ONE OF GOD'S MANY WONDER- FUL GIFTS TO BE USED IN THE SERVICE OF OTHERS. SO USE YOUR GIFT WELL.

—1 Peter 4:10 (Contemporary English Version)

We are all visitors to this time, this place. We are just passing through. Our purpose here is to observe, to learn, to grow, to love . . . and then we return home.

—Aboriginal proverb

THE WILL OF GOD WILL NEVER TAKE YOU WHERE THE GRACE OF GOD WILL NOT PROTECT YOU.

—Anonymous

[WHEN YOUR JOB IS DONE] WHAT YOU'RE LEFT IS FAMILY, FRIENDS, AND FAITH.

—Indra Nooyi

• •

All the goodness and the heroisms will rise up again, then be cut down again and rise up. It isn't that the evil thing wins—it never will—but that it doesn't die.

—John Steinbeck

The labyrinth provides the sacred space where the inner and outer worlds can commune, where the thinking mind and imaginative heart can flow together. It can provide a space to listen to our inner voice of wisdom and come to grips with our role in humankind's next evolutionary step.

—*Lauren Artress*

If you're not giving anything away, nothing new is going to come. Whether or not you keep the blessing depends on what you do with the blessing. When you're always lifting people, encouraging them, making them better, then blessings are always going to come to you.

—*Joel Osteen*

Remember, every single amazing thing you see, whether it is a building or technology or art, began as a dream in someone's mind.

—*Bill Pulte*

We are emissaries of hope when we give our focus to the present moment rather than to regrets of the past or concerns about the future.

—Joyce Rupp

• •

GIVE THANKS FOR UNKNOWN BLESSINGS ALREADY ON THEIR WAY.

—Native American saying

Character

• • • • • • • • • • •

Character may be manifested in the great moments, but it is made in the small ones.

—*Phillips Brooks*

• •

WHATEVER YOU CHOOSE TO DO, DO IT WITH INTEGRITY. IT IS THE MOST VALUABLE ASSET THAT YOU BRING TO A CAREER AND ULTIMATELY LEAVE WITH. IN THE END, IT IS THE ULTIMATE INSURANCE THAT YOU WILL NEVER HAVE TO LOOK BACK WITH REGRET.

—*Frank Biondi*

The seven deadly sins are:

1. Wealth without work.

2. Pleasure without conscience.

3. Knowledge without character.

4. Business without morality.

5. Science without humanity.

6. Worship without sacrifice.

7. Politics without principle.

—*Frederick Lewis Donaldson*

Face your deficien-
cies and acknowl-
edge them; but do
not let them master
you. Let them teach
you patience, sweet-
ness, insight.

—*Helen Keller*

• •

*The difference between
ordinary and extraordi-
nary is that little extra.*

—*Jimmy Johnson*

If you have men who will exclude any of God's creatures from the shelter of compassion and pity, you will have men who will deal likewise with their fellow men.

—*Saint Francis*

BEFORE YOU SPEAK, LET YOUR WORDS PASS THROUGH THREE GATES. AT THE FIRST GATE, ASK YOURSELF, IS IT TRUE? AT THE SECOND GATE ASK, IS IT NECESSARY? AT THE THIRD GATE ASK, IS IT KIND?

—*Attributed to Rūmī*

Search for the seed of good in every adversity. Master that principle and you will own a precious shield that will guard you well through all the darkest valleys you must traverse. Stars may be seen from the bottom of a deep well, when they cannot be discerned from the mountaintop. So will you learn things in adversity that you would never have discovered without trouble. There is always a seed of good. Find it and prosper.

—Og Mandino

It is not what you do for your children, but what you have taught them to do for themselves that will make them success-ful human beings.

—*Ann Landers*

• 19

Few things help an individual more than to place responsibility upon him, and to let him know that you trust him.

—*Booker T. Washington*

I ATTRIBUTE MY SUCCESS TO THIS: I NEVER GAVE OR TOOK AN EXCUSE.

—Florence Nightingale

• •

Of all the people you will know in a lifetime, you are the only one you will never leave nor lose. To the question of your life, you are the only answer. To the problems of your life, you are the only solution.

—Jo Coudert

Rebellion against your handicaps gets you nowhere. Self-pity gets you nowhere. One must have the adventurous daring to accept oneself as a bundle of possibilities and undertake the most interesting game in the world—making the most of one's best.

—**Harry Emerson Fosdick**

To put the world in order, we must first put the nation in order; to put the nation in order, we must first put the family in order; to put the family in order, we must first cultivate our personal life; we must first set our hearts right.

—*Confucius*

• •

MEN BECOME BUILDERS BY BUILDING AND LYRE-PLAYERS BY PLAYING THE LYRE; SO TOO WE BECOME JUST BY DOING JUST ACTS, TEMPERATE BY DOING TEMPERATE ACTS, BRAVE BY DOING BRAVE ACTS.

—*Aristotle*

Excellence is an art won by training and habituation: we do not act rightly because we have virtue or excellence, but we rather have these because we have acted rightly . . . We are what we repeatedly do. Excellence, then, is not an act but a habit.

— Will Durant paraphrasing Aristotle

● 23

This is true humility: not thinking less of ourselves but thinking of ourselves *less*.

—Rick Warren

Your best self can be found based on how you respond to failure.

—David Goggins

People are like stained-glass windows. They sparkle and shine when the sun is out, but when the darkness sets in, their true beauty is revealed only if there is a light from within.

—Elisabeth Kübler-Ross

Be aware of the actions you take and the consequences they have. It's easy to act in haste. It's easy to do selfish things. They may look good in the short term, but in the long term you'll be digging your own grave. The same goes for going after your passion. It may be hard in the short term, but it is more than worth it.

—**Unknown**

The object of education is to give man the unity of truth. Formerly, when life was simple, all the different elements of man were in complete harmony. But when there came the separation of the intellect from the spiritual and the physical, the school education put entire emphasis on the intellect and on the physical side of man. We devote our sole attention to giving children information, not knowing that by this emphasis we are accentuating a break between the intellectual, the physical, and the spiritual life.

—Rabindranath Tagore

The golden opportunity you are seeking is in yourself. It is not in your environment; it is not in luck or chance, or the help of others; it is in yourself alone.

—Orison Swett Marden

· 27

When you have respect for the elders, it extends to everything else, including all of nature and its life forms.

—Bear Heart

THE ONLY THING WE CAN DO IS HONESTLY LEARN FROM OUR FALLS.

—Ai Weiwei

We make a living by what we get, but we make a life by what we give.

—Unknown

The pain you feel today is the strength you feel tomorrow. In every challenge encountered there is opportunity for growth.

—Unknown

BELIEVE IN YOURSELF AND YOUR FEELINGS. TRUST YOURSELF TO DO WHAT YOUR HEART IS GUIDING YOU TO DO. YOUR INTUITION IS POWERFUL. TRUST IT.

—Unknown

We acquire the strength
we have overcome.

—*Ralph Waldo Emerson*

• •

Every choice you make has an end result.

—*Zig Ziglar*

Courage

• • • • • • • • • •

When you face your fears, you grow stronger. Each time you do something you're afraid of, it becomes easier. This has been true in my life, so I have no doubt that the same will be true for you. When you start out, it's hard, but it gets easier. Trust me.

—**Unknown**

Your strength is not in your muscles. It does not come from fighting negative situations or winning against a negative enemy. Your strength is in your calmness, in the clarity of your mind. Strength comes from putting the negative aside without reacting.

—Yogi Amrit Desai

THE MOST DIFFICULT THING IS THE DECISION TO ACT, THE REST IS MERELY TENACITY. THE FEARS ARE PAPER TIGERS. YOU CAN DO ANYTHING YOU DECIDE TO DO. YOU CAN ACT TO CHANGE AND CONTROL YOUR LIFE; AND THE PROCEDURE, THE PROCESS IS ITS OWN REWARD.

—Amelia Earhart

I SWORE NEVER TO BE SILENT WHENEVER WHEREVER HUMAN BEINGS ENDURE SUFFERING AND HUMILIATION. WE MUST TAKE SIDES. NEUTRALITY HELPS THE OPPRESSOR, NEVER THE VICTIM. SILENCE ENCOURAGES THE TORMEN-TOR, NEVER THE TORMENTED . . . ONE PERSON . . . ONE PER-SON OF INTEGRITY, CAN MAKE A DIFFERENCE, A DIFFERENCE OF LIFE AND DEATH.

—*Elie Wiesel*

To face your fears isn't a pleasant experience that anyone would consider a reward—it's much closer to being a punishment. Yet in the long run, many accomplishments in life come our way only if we overcome fear and acquire courage.

—Deepak Chopra

Great things will happen when you get up, dust your-self off, and go after life with determination and courage.

—Billy Cox

Overcome fear, behold wonder.

—Richard Bach

Be thankful for all the struggles you go through. They make you stronger, wiser and humble. Don't let it break you. Let it make you.

—Unknown

Each time a man stands up for an ideal, or acts to improve the lot of others, or strikes out against injustice, he sends forth a tiny ripple of hope, and crossing each other from a million different centers of energy and daring those ripples build a current which can sweep down the mightiest walls of oppression and resistance.

—Robert Francis Kennedy

YOU WILL BEGIN TO HEAL
WHEN YOU LET GO OF PAST
HURTS, FORGIVE THOSE WHO
HAVE WRONGED YOU, AND
LEARN TO FORGIVE YOURSELF
FOR YOUR MISTAKES.

—*Unknown*

• •

Defeat is never fatal.
Victory is never
final. It's courage
that counts.

—*Unknown*

He who is not courageous enough to take risks will accomplish nothing in life.

—Muhammad Ali

• 39

You have to be willing to take risks. I'm not talking about going for broke with a slim chance of success. I am talking about jumping into the unknown and going after the things that excite you, even if you are afraid.

—Debbie Millman

Whatever you do, you need courage. Whatever course you decide upon, there is always someone to tell you that you are wrong. There are always difficulties arising that tempt you to believe your critics are right. To map out a course of action and follow it to an end requires some of the same courage that a soldier needs. Peace has its victories, but it takes brave men and women to win them.

—**Ralph Waldo Emerson**

Creativity
and
Meaning

• • • • • • • • •

Challenges are what make life interesting and overcoming them is what makes life meaningful.

—*Attributed to Joshua J. Marine*

• •

Try not to become a man of success but rather try to become a man of value.

—*Albert Einstein*

Among our most univer-sal human longings is to affect the world with our actions somehow, to leave an imprint with our existence.

—Maria Popova

● 43

The creative person is, in any case, continually working at it . . . shuf-fling his information at all times, even when he is not conscious of it.

—Isaac Asimov

IT IS A FUNCTION OF
CREATIVE MEN TO
PERCEIVE THE RELATIONS
BETWEEN THOUGHTS,
OR THINGS, OR FORMS
OF EXPRESSION THAT
MAY SEEM UTTERLY
DIFFERENT, AND TO BE
ABLE TO COMBINE THEM
INTO SOME NEW FORM.

—*William Plomer*

Creativity is allow-ing yourself to make mistakes. Art is knowing which ones to keep.

—Scott Adams

· 45

ART IS THIS: CREATIVITY. IT'S JUST ANYTHING THAT'S DONE FOR ITS OWN SAKE.

—Naval Ravikant

Have a purpose, strive for its ful-
fillment. Strive to live in harmony
and cultivate loyalty, belief, and
faith. All of these are ingredients
that give substance to a full life.

—Bear Heart

• •

*We do not have a set
meaning programmed;
we are dynamic. Life is
meant to be lived.*

—Naval Ravikant

For the first time, most of humankind is in creative mode, not Samurai mode.

—*Akira the Don*

• 47

EITHER WRITE THINGS WORTH READING, OR DO THINGS WORTH THE WRITING.

—*Ben Franklin*

Escape competition through authenticity. Find the thing you know how to do better than anybody, because you are you. If you found your thing, you won't have competition.

—@loopuleasa, summarizing the words of Naval Ravikant

The most damaging
phrase in the language
is "We've always done
it this way!"

—*Grace Hopper*

· 49

**A human must
turn information
into intelligence or
knowledge. We've
tended to forget that
no computer will ever
ask a new question.**

—*Grace Hopper*

FIND OUT HOW MUCH GOOD YOU CAN DO IN THE WORLD ... IN A FORTHRIGHT, NOBLE, COURAGEOUS, EYES WIDE OPEN, ARTICULATE, EMBODIED MANNER.

—Jordan B. Peterson

• •

Dare to believe the whispers in your ears, that you might be meaningful, that one day you might change the world.

—Atticus

If you imagine less, less will be what you undoubtedly deserve. Do what you love, and don't stop until you get what you love. Work as hard as you can, imagine immensities, don't compromise, and don't waste time. Start now. Not 20 years from now, not two weeks from now. Now.

—Debbie Millman

*Creativity is just connecting things. When you ask creative people how they did something, they feel a little guilty because they didn't really **do** it, they just **saw** something. It seemed obvious to them after a while. That's because they were able to connect experiences they've had and synthesize new things. And the reason they were able to do that was that they've had more experiences or they have thought more about their experiences than other people.*

—Steve Jobs

Whatever you vividly imagine, ardently desire, sincerely believe, and enthusiastically act upon must inevitably come to pass.

—*Paul J. Meyer*

• 53

What do you wish to:

Tear up
     Give away
Burn
     Remove
Plant
     Sing
Create
     Wear?

—*Maria Harris*

WHAT MADE LEONARDO [DA VINCI] A GENIUS, WHAT SET HIM APART FROM PEOPLE WHO ARE MERELY EXTRAORDINARILY SMART, WAS CREATIVITY, THE ABILITY TO APPLY IMAGINATION TO INTELLECT . . . TO MAKE UNEXPECTED LEAPS THAT RELATED THINGS SEEN TO THINGS UNSEEN.

—*Walter Isaacson*

WHAT IS IT TOO SOON FOR, TOO LATE FOR, JUST THE RIGHT TIME FOR?

—*Dawna Markova*

When you are steeped in silence, when the world is elsewhere with its noise and motion, what are the sacred hungers that echo inside you?

—*Joyce Rupp*

Tell me, what is it you plan to do with your one wild and precious life?

—*Mary Oliver*

• •

Not everything that can be counted counts, and not everything that counts can be counted.

—**William Bruce Cameron**

Decide in your heart of hearts what really excites and challenges you, and start moving your life in that direction. Every decision you make, from what you eat to what you do with your time tonight, turns you into who you are tomorrow, and the day after that. Look at who you want to be, and start sculpting yourself into that person. You may not get exactly where you thought you'd be, but you will be doing things that suit you in a profession you believe in. Don't let life randomly kick you into the adult you don't want to become.

—Chris Hadfield

YOU CAN BECOME BLIND BY SEEING EACH DAY AS A SIMILAR ONE. EACH DAY IS A DIFFERENT ONE, EACH DAY BRINGS A MIRACLE OF ITS OWN. IT'S JUST A MATTER OF PAYING ATTENTION TO THIS MIRACLE.

—*Paulo Coelho*

• •

Train yourself to listen to that small voice that tells us what's important and what's not.

—*Sue Grafton*

Life's not about expecting, hoping and wishing, it's about doing, being and becoming. It's about the choices you've just made, and the ones you're about to make; it's about the things you choose to say—today. It's about what you're gonna do after you finish reading this.

—*Attributed to Mike Dooley*

THERE ARE MANY THINGS
IN LIFE THAT WILL CATCH
YOUR EYE, BUT ONLY A
FEW WILL CATCH YOUR
HEART. PURSUE THOSE.

—*Michael Nolan*

• •

Ordinary riches can be stolen
from a man. Real riches cannot.
In the treasury-house of your
soul, there are infinitely precious
things, that may not be taken
from you.

—*Oscar Wilde*

We are each gifted in a unique and important way. It is our privilege and our adventure to discover our own special light.

—**Evelyn Mary Dunbar**

If you have anything really valuable to contribute to the world, it will come through the expression of your own personality—that single spark of divinity that sets you off and makes you different from every other living creature.

—**Bruce Barton**

Human beings come to this world to do particular work. That work is the purpose, and each is specific to the person.

—*Rūmī*

• •

Creativity is equal parts of thought and action.

—*Ginny Ruffner*

IF YOU LOOK AT THE COMPONENTS OF LONG-TERM WELL-BEING, IT HAS NOTHING TO DO WITH MATERIAL GOODS. ONCE YOU'RE PAST A CERTAIN LEVEL OF MATERIAL WELL-BEING, PEOPLE'S LONG-TERM HAPPINESS AND WELL-BEING IS ABOUT HAVING DEEP PERSONAL RELATIONSHIPS, BELIEVING IN SOMETHING LARGER THAN THEMSELVES, AND DOING SOMETHING MEANINGFUL THAT THEY ENJOY.

—Daniel Pink

Determination

· · · · · · · · · · · · · · · · · · ·

All things that are worthwhile are very difficult to obtain.

—*Jonny Kim*

● ●

We decide if our stumbling blocks become stepping stones.

—*Jessica Flanigan*

ABILITY IS WHAT YOU'RE CAPABLE OF DOING. MOTIVATION DETERMINES WHAT YOU DO. ATTITUDE DETERMINES HOW WELL YOU DO IT.

—Lou Holtz

You simply can't afford to wait for either perfect conditions or the perfect plan. Goal setting is often a matter of balancing timing against available resources. Opportunities are easily missed by holding off for the exact right moment.

—Gary Ryan Blair

**After the final no
there comes a yes**

**And on that yes the
future world depends.**

— *Wallace Stevens*

• •

*The challenges in
our lives are there
to STRENGTHEN
our CONVICTIONS.
They are NOT there to
run us over.*

— *Nick Vujicic*

[The] only thing that matters is what you say to yourself. A person with a vision continues when confronted with obstacles . . . A lot of people put motivational quotes up on the wall and all they do is collect dust. Become what that quote says. Live it every day.

—*David Goggins*

LIFE IS REALLY A SINGLE-PLAYER GAME. IT'S ALL GOING ON [IN] YOUR HEAD, YOU KNOW. WHATEVER YOU THINK YOU BELIEVE WILL VERY MUCH SHAPE YOUR REALITY.

—Naval Ravikant

● ●

If I fail, I try again, and again, and again. If YOU fail, are you going to try again? The human spirit can handle much worse than we realize. It matters HOW you are going to FINISH. Are you going to finish strong?

—Nick Vujicic

A CLEAR MIND
LEADS TO BETTER
JUDGMENT AND
BETTER OUTCOMES.
A HAPPY, CALM,
AND PEACEFUL
PERSON WILL MAKE
BETTER DECISIONS.
SO IF YOU WANT TO
OPERATE AT PEAK
PERFORMANCE,
YOU HAVE TO
LEARN HOW TO
TAME YOUR MIND.

—*Naval Ravikant*

One definition of a winner is someone who never let losing stop them.

—*Jordan B. Peterson*

• •

Never give up. This may be your moment for a miracle.

—*Greg Anderson*

NEVER GIVE UP 5 MINUTES BEFORE THE MIRACLE. ONCE YOU COMMIT TO AN IDEA, MAKE ADJUSTMENTS AS YOU GAIN INFORMATION, BUT HANG IN THERE. MOST OF YOUR COMPETITION WILL GIVE UP BEFORE YOU DO!

—*Bill Pulte*

I often tell young kids, and particularly my grandkids, don't ever count yourself out. You'll never know how good you are unless you try. Dream the impossible and go out and make it happen. I walked on the moon. What can't you do?

—*Eugene Cernan*

• •

It's often possible to turn negative situations into positive. Never feel a situation is all negative. There's a counterpart that is positive. Look for it, reach for it, utilize it—it will offset the negative.

—*Bear Heart*

Part of playing sports is just staying in the moment. You know, we always say "one play at a time." You can't make up for things that have happened in the past. You've just got to think about what you're going to do moving forward.

—**Tom Brady**

Intelligence and ambition help. Grit and hustle are a prerequisite.

Many have the first two. Fewer have the second set. But what about the ability to get your ass beat, lose, and rise from the ashes?

F*** who's still standing. I wanna know who gets back up after being dropped.

—*Ed Latimore*

We don't have an eternity to realize our dreams, only the time we are here.

—Susan Taylor

· 77

THERE IS NOTHING WE CANNOT LIVE DOWN, AND RISE ABOVE, AND OVERCOME.

—Ella Wheeler Wilcox

When you get into a tight place, and everything goes against you till it seems as if you couldn't hold on a minute longer, *never give up then*, for that's just the place and time that the tide'll turn.

—*Harriet Beecher Stowe*

I've failed over and over and over again in my life. And that is why I succeed.

—*Michael Jordan*

Independence

· · · · · · · · · · · · · · · ·

IT'S YOUR PLACE IN THE WORLD; IT'S YOUR LIFE. GO ON AND DO ALL YOU CAN WITH IT, AND MAKE IT THE LIFE YOU WANT TO LIVE.

—Mae Jemison

• •

Institutions don't change the world in fundamental ways. The way the world changes is heart to heart to heart by individuals, not by institutions.

—Ram Dass

Build your own dreams, or someone else will hire you to build theirs.

—Farrah Gray

· ·

Freedom of speech and freedom of action are meaningless without freedom to think. And there is no freedom of thought without doubt.

—Bergen Evans

Our life is what our thoughts make it.

—Marcus Aurelius

• •

Great spirits have always encountered violent opposition from mediocre minds.

—Albert Einstein

EACH OF US IS
RESPONSIBLE FOR
SETTING THE TONE OF
OUR LIVES. WE CREATE
OUR OWN REALITY BY
HOW WE CHOOSE TO
THINK, SPEAK, AND
RESPOND TO THE
PEOPLE/CHALLENGES/
HAPPENINGS/BLESSINGS
IN OUR LIVES.

—Kerri Walsh Jennings

Joy

..

When I stand before God at the end of my life, I would hope that I would not have a single bit of talent left and could say, "I used everything you gave me."

—*Erma Bombeck*

• •

Peace is happiness at rest, and happiness is peace in motion.

—*Naval Ravikant*

Unless your heart, your soul, and your whole being are behind every decision you make, the words from your mouth will be empty, and each action will be meaningless. Truth and confidence are the roots of happiness.

—*Anonymous*

There is a story in every thing, and every being, and every moment, were we alert to catch it, were we ready with our tender nets . . .

—**Brian Doyle**

• •

Life always bursts the boundaries of formulas.

—**Antoine de Saint-Exupéry**

Go live and be great today. In order for your someday to become reality, you've just got to be your best today.

—Dabo Swinney

YOU FIGURE OUT WHAT MAKES YOU LAUGH, AND YOU DO MORE OF IT. YOU LEARN WHAT MAKES YOU CRY, AND YOU DO LESS OF IT.

—Mandy Hale

Leadership

• • • • • • • • • • • •

Great leaders are idealists.
They are optimists. They
overestimate what we are
capable of and inspire us
to believe the same.

—*Simon Sinek*

• •

**Leadership is actually
more akin to consistency
of authenticity across
stressful environments
. . . We trust people when
we know how they're
going to show up.**

—*Michael Gervais*

BECAUSE POWER COR-
RUPTS, SOCIETY'S DEMANDS
FOR MORAL AUTHORITY AND
CHARACTER INCREASE AS
THE IMPORTANCE OF THE
POSITION INCREASES.

—*John Adams*

• •

If your actions create a legacy
that inspires others to dream
more, learn more, do more
and become more, then you
are an excellent leader.

—*Dolly Parton*

Authenticity is the alignment of head, mouth, heart, and feet—thinking, saying, feeling, and doing the same thing—consistently. This builds trust, and followers **love** leaders they can trust.

—**Lance Secretan**

Mindfulness must be engaged. Once there is seeing, there must be acting. Otherwise, what is the use of seeing?

—**Thich Nhat Hanh**

What everyone knows is what has already happened or become obvious. What the aware individual knows is what has not yet taken shape, what has not yet occurred. Everyone says victory in battle is good, but if you see the subtle and notice the hidden so as to seize victory where there is no form, this is really good.

—*Zhang Yu*

WHEN YOUR STRATEGY IS
DEEP AND FAR-REACHING,
THEN WHAT YOU GAIN BY
YOUR CALCULATIONS IS MUCH,
SO YOU CAN WIN BEFORE
YOU EVEN FIGHT. WHEN YOUR
STRATEGIC THINKING IS SHAL-
LOW AND NEARSIGHTED, THEN
WHAT YOU GAIN BY YOUR CAL-
CULATIONS IS LITTLE, SO YOU
LOSE BEFORE YOU DO BATTLE.

—*Zhang Yu*

Only people of inner authority ... will use the outer authority correctly.

—*Richard Rohr*

The most successful people don't live in the past or the future. They have an incredible ability to focus and live fully in the present. No wasted energy on regret or fear.

—*Bill Mitchell*

THE WORLD IS LITTERED WITH ONCE-GREAT THINGS THAT DETERIORATED AND FAILED; ONLY A RARE FEW HAVE KEPT REINVENTING THEMSELVES TO GO ON TO NEW HEIGHTS OF GREATNESS.

—*Ray Dalio*

To find the real leader, search where the fight is hardest.

—*Wesley King*

Great leaders gather information but also lead by intuition and instinct. Opportunity often knocks at inopportune times. You must be ready to trust your gut and commit to action.

—*Unknown*

Love

• • • •

The most wonderful
of all things in life, I
believe, is the discovery
of another human
being with whom
one's relationship
has a glowing depth,
beauty, and joy as the
years increase. This
inner progressiveness
of love between two
human beings is a most
marvellous thing.

—Sir Hugh Walpole

Even
After
All this time
The sun never says to the earth,

"You owe
Me."

Look
What happens
With a love like that,
It lights the
Whole
Sky.

—Ḥāfiẕ, as translated by Daniel Ladinsk

TO FALL IN LOVE IS EASY,
EVEN TO REMAIN IN IT
IS NOT DIFFICULT; OUR
HUMAN LONELINESS IS
CAUSE ENOUGH. BUT IT IS A
HARD QUEST WORTH MAK-
ING TO FIND A COMRADE
THROUGH WHOSE STEADY
PRESENCE ONE BECOMES
STEADILY THE PERSON ONE
DESIRES TO BE.

—Anna Louise Strong

There are two sides to most every situation in life. Try to balance them out…

Among the Navajo, when a man attends an event or council where an opinion must be formed, he is accompanied by his wife or eldest daughter. They say that because men and women see things differently, a balanced opinion can only be formed by a man and woman together.

—*Bear Heart*

OLD FRIENDS CANNOT BE CREATED OUT OF HAND. NOTHING CAN MATCH THE TREASURE OF COMMON MEMORIES, OF TRIALS ENDURED TOGETHER, OF QUARRELS AND RECONCILIATIONS AND GENEROUS EMOTIONS.

—*Antoine de Saint-Exupéry*

The art of being yourself at your best is the art of unfolding your personality into the person you want to be . . . Be gentle with yourself, learn to love yourself, to forgive yourself, for only as we have the right attitude toward ourselves can we have the right attitude toward others.

— Wilferd Peterson

Work

. . . . .

Work for someone who believes in you—because when they believe in you, they'll invest in you.

—*Marissa Mayer*

• •

What you do, who you do it with and how you do it are way more important than how hard you work.

—*Naval Ravikant*

If you're offered a seat on a rocket ship, don't ask what seat! Just get on.

—Sheryl Sandberg

BECOME THE BEST IN THE WORLD AT WHAT YOU DO. KEEP REDEFINING WHAT YOU DO UNTIL THIS IS TRUE.

—Naval Ravikant

Never hire or promote in your own image. It is foolish to replicate your strength. It is stupid to replicate your weakness. Employ, trust, and reward those whose perspective, ability, and judgment are radically different from your own and recognize that it requires uncommon humility, tolerance, and wisdom.

—Dee Hock

There's a huge power in inexperience. You just don't know what's impossible, and therefore think, "Of course this can be done!"

— Wendy Kopp

When your gut instinct is very, very strong, you've got to go with your gut.

— Cathy Lanier

PICK BUSINESS PARTNERS WITH HIGH INTELLIGENCE, ENERGY, AND, ABOVE ALL, INTEGRITY.

—Naval Ravikant

• •

If a man can write a better book, preach a better sermon or make a better rat trap than his neighbor: though he build his house in the woods, the world will make a beaten track to his door.

—Omni Grove Park Inn (Asheville, North Carolina) quote at entrance door

From this day forward, Flight Control will be known by two words: "Tough and Competent." **Tough** means we are forever accountable for what we do or what we fail to do. We will never again compromise our responsibilities . . . **Competent** means we will never take anything for granted . . . These words are the price of admission to the ranks of Mission Control.

—*Gene Kranz, speech given to Mission Control after Apollo 1 ground disaster*

Pick an industry where you can play long-term games with long-term people . . . Embrace accountability, and take business risks under your own name. Society will reward you with responsibility, equity, and leverage.

—*Naval Ravikant*

LIFE ALWAYS GIVES US EXACTLY THE TEACHER WE NEED AT EVERY MOMENT ... EVERY MOMENT IS THE GURU.

—Joan Tollifson

Life is precious—do not waste it doing anything that your heart does not respect or agree with.

—Attributed to Leon Brown

Work at its best involves a flow state where time stands still and you can feel present, involved in the process of the work itself, and be satisfied that you are creating something good, using your skills to their utmost.

Work aligned with your purpose is optimal.

Work should contribute to something greater than yourself or your family—it should fulfill your purpose on earth and contribute in a way only you can.

Work should allow continual opportunities for growth; if you are not allowed to grow anymore, then you need to find new work or a new workplace.

Work should not require you to compromise your integrity.

—M.C. Sungaila

Work changes into service when we view it as more than something that has to be done, when it becomes a way for our authentic self to transmit integrity, kindness, and justice.

—**Joyce Rupp**

Learn to sell. Learn to build. If you can do both, you will be unstoppable.

—**Naval Ravikant**

DREAM BIG, WORK HARD, STAY FOCUSED, AND SURROUND YOURSELF WITH GOOD PEOPLE.

—Unknown

About
the
Author

•••••••

M.C. Sungaila lives in Orange County, California, where she practices law and writes regularly. She is the creator of the Mother's Thoughts for the Day series and is known to post inspiring quotes on her refrigerator at home and computer at work.

CPSIA information can be obtained
at www.ICGtesting.com
Printed in the USA
JSHW020458301020
9191JS00003B/9